# MOSTAR

## THE LIGHT OF MOSTAR

*W*hen a man stays overnight in Mostar, it is not the sound that wakes him up but the light. I know this from my own experience. The light welcomed me when I arrived, followed me during my stay from morning to evening, and later, after I had departed, it stayed in me as the main characteristic of my memory of Mostar. It always seemed to me that what shines above your naturally privileged town and what permeates everything in it is some special illumination, exceptional in strength and quality. I have always thought that, with it, love of life, courage and serenity, a sense of proportion and creative work must have entered Mostar man.

I was never able to take my fill of this light although I met it everywhere: in the laughter of your people and the clear vowels of their speech, on the faces of the young boys and girls as they strolled early of an evening. It is iridescent like the golden, restless reflection in a glass of Žilavka from Mostar, it lives as through a charged strength and deliciousness in your peaches and cherries. It is hidden in the cool cold water from the Radobolja. It makes the Neretva your brightest river, it gives an elemental magnitude even to the bare Karst of your surrounding hills. It shines through the stories of the people of Mostar relating the struggle for their present freedom and today's efforts for progress in every direction.

I remember Mostar best for this light.

Ivo Andrić

*Series*
TOURISM AND HERITAGE
No 22

ISBN 953-215-029-3

*Editors*
Ana Ivelja-Dalmatin
Mili Bijavica
Mato Njavro
Marija Vranješ
Milan Vukelić
Jasna Vukšić

*Editor-in-Chief*
Mato Njavro

*Art editor*
Milan Vukelić

*Publisher*
Turistička naklada d.o.o., Zagreb
Fortunatrade tours d.o.o., Mostar

*For Publisher*
Marija Vranješ
Mili Bijavica

*Prepress*
Sibi, Zagreb

*Photolithographs*
Denona, d.o.o. Zagreb

*Print*
Vjesnik d.d., Zagreb

# MOSTAR
## AND SURROUNDINGS

History • Culture • Art
Natural beauties • Tourism

*The Old Bridge at night*

**Text**
ALIJA BIJAVICA
MATO NJAVRO

**Translator**
Živan Filippi

**English language editor**
Celia Irving

**Photos**
Vjekoslav Bubalo
Sulejman Demirović
Arhiv Turističke naklade

Zagreb, 2004.

# MOSTAR – AN AREA RICH IN CULTURE AND CONTACTS OF CIVILISATION

*M*ostar is the economic, political and cultural centre of Herzegovina. It lies in the large Mostar basin at a height of 60 m above sea-level, at the crossroads of lowland- and mountainous Herzegovina.

It is surrounded by the slopes of the mountains of Prenj, Velež, and Čabulje, and the hills of Hum. Not far from the Mostar basin is Bijelo polje to the north and Bišće polje to the south. The main river in Herzegovina, the Nereva, flows through the centre of the town, dividing it in two; on the right side is the larger and more developed area, and on the left a steeper and smaller section.

A modern highway follows the Neretva valley connecting Sarajevo and Mostar with the Adriatic Sea, together with the electric railway. The Neretva, as part of the Mostar basin, fills the accumulative lakes of Jablanica, Grabovica, Salakovci and Vrapčići with water. The river bank gets wider and lower before Mostar, but then flows through Mostar cutting a canyon and creating, near the Old Bridge, its most beautiful scenery, something no visitor ever for-

*Mostar, a town of modern architecture*

⇦ *The single-arch Old Bridge in Mostar dating from 1566*

gets. The clear and clean rivulet of Radobolja joins the Neretva next to the Old Bridge on the right.

In the 15th century, even before Turkish times, a small settlement, a nucleus of the Old Town, began to develop on the left bank of the Neretva around a bridge that hung on chains. Taking into consideration the value of the bridge as an important means of communication, this settlement developed fairly quickly and soon took over the importance of the ancient town of Blagaj. In the middle of the 15th century (in 1477), Mostar had 19 houses. According to documents

from Dubrovnik's archives, Vlatko, the son of Stjepan Herceg Vukčić-Kosača, was in command of the towers around the bridge from July 2, 1452.

The Turks occupied this settlement, as well as Blagaj, during 1466 or 1467, or, at latest, in 1468. They gave it the name of Köprü hisar – the fortification on the bridge. The name "Mostar" was mentioned in 1474 for the first time. The guards of the chain bridge were in the towers on both sides of the Neretva bridge and were called "mostari" (mentioned for the first time in 1440 and the town is presumed to have got its

*Mostar, the Old Bridge, a masterpiece of Turkish architecture*

⇦ *Mostar, the town built on both banks of the River Neretva*

*The beauty of the Neretva and the unique riparian architecture*

name after them).

During the time of Turkish rule Mostar became the seat of both civil and military officials and dignitaries. "Čaršija" developed around the new stone bridge (today's Old Bridge), which was built in 1566 in the vicinity of the chain bridge. It had several towers, gates, a mosque, restaurants and numerous craft workshops. This well preserved oriental part of the town attracts not only tourists but also artists, poets and other chance travellers, and all of them wish to come back to enjoy its uniqueness. Mostar is always young, unique, and unforgettable.

The seat of the diocese of Sarsiteron, founded at the council of Solin in 533, was in the broader area of Mostar (in the present day settlement of Cim where the remains of a late Byzantine basilica were discovered). Mostar has been the seat of the Orthodox metropolitan bishop

*Rugmaking, the skill of handicraftsmen, rich colours and decorations*

since 1767, and since 1847 of the Catholic bishop as well.

Mostar, the most developed economic centre of Herzegovina, together with its surroundings, has rich agriculture, especially wine-growing with the famous quality wines of Herzegovina, Žilavka and Blatina. Metal-working, textiles, tobacco and building industries are also well-developed, as well as communications, trade, catering, and tourism.

Mostar is surely a town in which the influences of East and West have been harmoniously interwoven.

*Kujundžiluk, the old town of Mostar ("čaršija") on the left bank of the Neretva*

*Kujundžiluk and the Old Bridge, unique architectural examples of Oriental culture*

*The amazing lights on the left bank of the Neretva*

*The picturesque ambience of the old town ("čaršija")*

Mostar, *"a town of stone on stone"*

# CLIMATE AND GEOGRAPHY

*T*he grey-green river Neretva flows through Mostar and lower limestone hills towards the sea, while the warm Mediterranean air penetrates from the Adriatic sea to the village of Prigrađani above Mostar, under the Prenj mountain, and farther on towards the north.

The influence of the Mediterranean climate creates favourable conditions for the cultivation of various southerly crops so that Mostar and its near surroundings, especially the Nereta valley, are rich in tropical fruit, vegetables and other Mediterranean plants.

The high quality Herzegovina tobacco and grapes are cultivated together with various sorts of early vegetables and fruit, especially cherries, apricots, figs and peaches.

It is well known that the famous Herzegovina wines Žilavka and Blatina were produced in ancient times.

Mostar, a town existing on both sides of the Neretva, is located 43°21' latitude north and 17°49' longitude east. It has a Mediterranean climate with mild winters and warm long summers. The average annual temperature is around 15° C; in winter it is higher on average than 5° C, while in summer it is higher than 25° C. Although the Velež mountain above Mostar (1967 m above sea level) has snow even in summer, it rarely snows down in the town, and if it falls it melts very quickly.

*In summer months the clear Neretva is suitable for swimming*

*The mild climate is ideal for Mediterranean crops, especially for wine and tobacco growing*

# OLD SETTLEMENTS

*T*he oldest quarter – "mahala", formed by the Turks after the occupation of Mostar, was called Sinan-pasha's mahala. It is evident from surviving documents of the Mostar quadi from 1631 that Mostar had 24 mahalas with 22 mosques. The town expanded in the 17th century gaining even more mahalas plus the market-place ("čaršija") near the Old Bridge. The Emperor's Čaršija was also built then. During Turkish rule it was the main square where they read orders to the people and gave them necessary information coming from the government in Istanbul or from the local authorities in Mostar. Town-criers ("telali") publicised the buying and selling of property and real estate, publicised auctions and called the people to war. Sports competitions in wrestling, long jump, throwing stone took place in the square, as well as various entertainments during religious feast days.

*Mostar and its beautiful river Neretva*

*Mostar has kept its ancient roots with both harmony and beauty*

*Mostar, a town open to new vistas* ⇨

# TRADE AND HANDICRAFTS IN TURKISH TIMES

*T*he ancient caravan routes passed through Mostar along which the cargoes of salt, fish, olive oil, dried figs, linen and other goods were transported from Dubrovnik, Kotor, Gabela and other littoral towns, while cargoes of cereals, honey, wax, tallow, wool, meat, etc. were going from the mainland towards the sea.

Caravanserais were built for merchants and drovers, and also for their goods and horses. Today, they represent an historic heritage, as many other buildings from the Ottoman period do.

Although a strong earthquake affected Mostar in the 16th century, together with the plague which raged twice in the same century, the town managed to overcome all the difficulties and continue to develop. Indeed, Mostar recovered even after the third epidemic of plague, which claimed many lives at the beginning of the 18th century.

Handicrafts were very much developed even in the 16th century. Today's old part of the town on the left bank of the Neretva, was called Kujundžiluk after the numerous coppersmiths ("kujundžije"). There were many tailors ("terzije"), but the most numerous artisans were tanners ("tabaci"), with their workshops on the left bank, next to the very confluence of the Radobolja and Neretva. Tanners, great masters for processing leather, were well organised in guilds ("esnafi").

*Kujundžiluk, the old town ("čaršija") which owes its name to the goldsmiths ("kujundžije")*

*Kujundžiluk, an area of small artisan workshops and fascinating handicrafts*

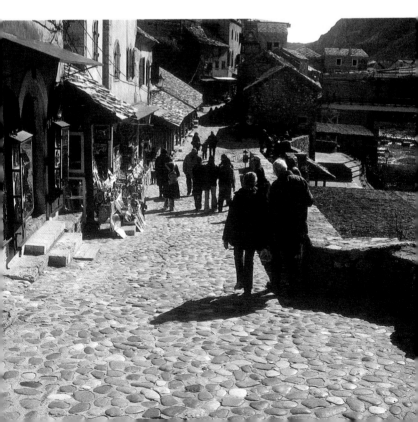

# THE HISTORY OF MOSTAR

*F*ertile fields along the Neretva, a pleasant climate and rich possibilities for trapping and fishing enabled prehistoric man from the Palaeolithic Age to settle in the location of Mostar and its surroundings. There are only rare remains from that period, so that the site at Badanj near Stolac is of great importance in witnessing the existence of man in the area of Mostar in this oldest period of human history.

Another valuable site which indicates the life of man in the distant past is in the immediate vicinity of Mostar. This is the Green Cave (Zelena Pećina) near Blagaj. There are also individual finds all over the surroundings of Mostar.

Every chance traveller is amazed by the numerous hill-forts on both sides of the Neretva. They belong mostly to the Bronze and Iron Ages and suggest that this area was

*The archaeological site of Badanj, the oldest human habitation known in the valley of the Bregava river (12000 to 16000 BC)*

*Blagaj, Tekija, a centuries-old settlement of dervishes and the source of the river Buna*

*One of numerous hill-forts dating from Illyrian times*

*Počitelj*

densely populated in these periods.

Previous to and during Hellenic times, Mostar and its surroundings were incorporated into the most advanced Illyrian small state of the tribe of Daorsi, who were ahead of the development level of other Illyrian tribes. Therefore, they often took sides with the Greeks and Romans in their conflicts with neighbouring tribes and their plundering ways of life. The remains of towns have been found in several places in the area of Daorson to the west as far as Zvonigrad in Mostarsko Blato. The ancient Greek and later Roman cultures found fertile soil here for their development and they flourished more than in other regions of Bosnia and Herzegovina.

The Romans arrived in this area as allies of the Daorsi rather early, even in the 2nd century BC. How-ever, there are no more significant remains of their culture before the pacification of this province by the Romans in the year 6 AD. The Romans began to build towns and settlements and link them by roads as early as the first century AD. The find at Dretelj shows that Christianity came to the Neretva valley during the persecution of Christians. It flourished here as nowhere else in the territory of Bosnia and Herzegovina. Archaeological maps depict numerous church buildings in the area from Bijelo Polje to Čapljina. The most important finds are in the town of Mostar, a basilica in Cim, and churches in Žitomislić, which are of world significance on a global scale. It was normal for this area to have its own diocese at that time, which was called *Sarsenterensis,* and the majority of historians and archaeologists consider that its see was in today's Mostar. On the other hand, some think that its see was in Žitomislić or Stolac, and that the diocese of Martaritana had its see in Mostar. There are villages today which still have names after the churches of that time, i.e. after their saints (Sutina = St John, Žuranj = St George, Mogorjelo = St Hermagora – Mogor, etc.).

The great movement of the peoples devastated the province. It was ended by the arrival of the Croats at the invitation of the Roman Emperor Heraclius to fight against the Avars, which was later chronicled by the 10th C Emperor Constantine Porphyrogenitus. An autonomous province, called Hum Land, Hum or Zahumlje, was formed in the areas of the ancient small state of the Daorsi tribe. Its seat was in the area of Mostar at the beginning. Emperor Porphyrogenitus mentioned two cities: Bona (Blagaj), and on the other side of the river, Hum, which many consider to be the town in the area of Mostar. Ston, later on, took over the role of the seat of the Hum rulers and bishops, but Mostar continued to play the role of an area of great importance. Mostar kept its role even when an autonomous province, later called Herzegovina, was created within the Bosnian state, and nominally under the supreme rule of Croatian-Hungarian kings. This was at the time of Kosač, Sandalj Hranić and his nephew Stjepan Vukčić. Many of our uplands are full of the remains of the towns and towers of that time built until the fall of the Turks. Blagaj, Herceg's town, is

*Počitelj, a medieval fortified town on the left bank of the Neretva*

*Mogorjelo, the remains of a villa rustica from Roman times*

*Mogorjelo, a detail of a wine-cellar from the 4th C AD*

especially important. Historical sources reveal other more important centres in the area of Mostar, for example Cim Town, the settlement of Mosti in the area of Cim and Old Bridge. Počitelj, which was built by the men of Dubrovnik at the time of the Croatian-Hungarian King Matijaš, also played a significant role as a defence fortification against the Turks. The glory of the ancient Hum Land and later Herzegovina was then eclipsed by Turkish occupation from 1463 to 1472.

The Turks occupied Mostar in 1468. Due to its strategic importance the town expanded quickly. Handicrafts and trade developed and the town became the cultural and educational centre of this part of the Ottoman Empire, whose economic system was based on feudal estates, landowners and serfs.

The first "mejdan"-square was built not far from the bridge. Sinan, the governor of the province, erected the mosque and public baths ("hamam") in 1475. Houses of oriental architecture lined the steep banks of the Neretva around "mejdan", with their courtyards ("avlije") full of flowers. Karađozbeg was the donator of the most important Mostar mosque erected in 1577 together with the religious school ("medresa").

Guilds built the market-place Kujundžiluk on both sides of the bridge. Mostar had 1,000 houses and about 12,000 inhabitants in the 17th century. About thirty crafts were active in more than 300 shops. Some of them achieved very high quality. The Turkish Empire, when expanding, built monumental buildings, among which Koski Mehmed-pasha's mosque (in 1619), Roznamedži-Ibrahim efendi's mosque and the aqueduct (1629-30), Ćejvan-Ćehaj's mosque (1552), which is the oldest surviving mosque in the town, Nasuh-aga Vučaković's mosque (before 1558), Tabačica mosque, Ćejvan-beg's hamam (1658), Kriva Ćuprija (before 1558), Sahat-kula,,, Later on more simple buildings were built, and the Turks permitted the renovation of the old Orthodox church (in 1833), and the building of a new one in 1873); also the building of a Roman-Catholic church, and many other valuable buildings. Turkish power decreased after their defeat near Vienna in 1683, while their feudal system was torn apart by internal conflicts, as the consequence of a weaker economy, and frequent Venetian attacks.

Even before the arrival of the first printing house, founded by f. Frano

Miličević in 1872, the learned men of Mostar wrote literary and calligraphic works. The most outstanding writer was Mustafa Ljubović-Šeh Jujo. The Turks also printed the newspaper "Neretva" in Turkish (in 1876).

### Turkish Rule and its Decline

Mostar was under Turkish occupation from 1468 to 1878 when Austro-Hungarian occupation took place. The Venetians also attacked it frequently both from the west and the south, and especially during the Candian war of 1652.

Ottoman power began to decline after the third siege of Vienna in 1683, when the Polish army under the command of Jan Sobjeski defeated the Turks. Rebellions against the Turks became frequent in all parts of their empire.

Rebellions against high taxes took place in the middle of the 18th century and later as well. Under these pressures the Turks allowed Mostar to build an Orthodox

church in 1833, and a Catholic one in 1864. The new Orthodox church was completed in 1873.

The old oriental milieu of Mostar began to feel the influence of a modern administration, after the Austro-Hungarian occupation of 1878. The railway was introduced as the basis for a new economic development. However the changes in the

*Mostar, Karađoz-bey's mosque built in 1557*

*Mostar, a hammam in the Priječka čaršija built in the 16th C*

economy were not considerable because the railway and the tobacco factory could not alter the feudal relationships in the country and the habitual handicrafts in Mostar and other towns.

Educational and cultural societies were active and various newspapers and three periodicals were printed in three printing-houses. Mostar became a cultural centre by gathering well-known writers around the periodical "Zora" edited by the poets Šantić, Dučić and Ćorović. The following Croatian newspapers were printed in f. Frane Miličević's printing-house: "Hercegovački bosiljak" (1883 – 1884), "Novi hercegovački bosiljak" (1884 – 1885), "Glas Hercegovine" (1885 – 1896), "Osvit" (1898 – 1907), "Franjevački glasnik" (1899 – 1901)... Theatre life was also very rich due to active amateurs and frequent performances of respectable visiting theatre groups.

Two tall concrete bridges were erected over the Neretva in the new part of the town, next to the railway line. The comfortable hotel "Neretva", Public Baths, the Grammar School with the Elementary School next to it, buildings of the town administration, new merchant streets, the introduction of electricity – all this gave a new appearance to the town, although Austrian architecture clashed with the old oriental architecture.

Mostar had between 14,000 and 15,000 inhabitants before the Second World War. Industrial workers were not numerous; mostly miners in the coal mines and textile workers in a small textile factory. After the Second World War, Mostar became the centre of the aluminium industry, the aircraft industry ("Soko"), the industry of textile products; also an important centre for the production of tobacco, grapes, fruit and seasonal vegetables, which were grown on plantations and produced in factories.

The new conflicts of 1992/1995 took more than 2,000 lives and 26,000 refugees escaped to foreign countries (according to the data of the European Union). More than 5,000 buildings in the interior of the town were destroyed. Industry, infrastructure and many historical and

*Mostar, the old Orthodox church built in 1834*

cultural buildings were devastated. Institutions deteriorated and the standard of living decreased considerably. The town was divided into two parts (Croatian and Muslim) by the "division line".

The European Union established an administration in Mostar immediately after signing the general peace agreement and the end of military conflict (in July 1994). Both local parties signed the Memorandum of Understanding. The mutual aim was to unite the town again, to create freedom of movement, shared police forces, to enable the return of refugees and exiled citizens. After organising Bosnia and Herzegovina as a modern state based on Western European democratic principles, and including it in the international political and economic associations, Mostar should have all the conditions for an intensive development

*Mostar, the Catholic church built in 1866 with the Franciscan monastery next to it - destroyed in the war of 1992/1995 and since rebuilt*

and much better future, being one of the important regional centres of Bosnia and Herzegovina.

*Mostar, the Tobacco Factory*

*Mostar is the seat of the aluminium industry*

# CULTURAL AND HISTORICAL HERITAGE

Situated at the crossroads of East and West, Mostar was exposed to various influences which were reflected in many features of the life here. The Turks developed it, trying to adapt their building art to this ambience and introducing oriental styles of building. Almost from the beginning, Mostar was a place where the cultures of the Orient and the West, the mainland and the Adriatic Sea, met and influenced each other. Various invaders tried to destroy it

*The calm beauty of the Neretva roofed over by the Old Bridge*

but also to build it again; they came and went. Every historical period has left the mark of its duration here.

**The Old Bridge** – When the Turks invaded Mostar, there was a wooden bridge near today's Old Bridge; it hung on chains, and the Turks used it for some time. As it became worn out in the middle of the 16th century, the people of Mostar asked the authorities in Istanbul to build a new bridge from quality material. The Old Bridge was completed and put into service in July or August 1566. It was designed by the builder Hajrudin, pupil of the famous Sinan, the great Turkish architect of the 16th century. Its span is 28,70 meters and it has only one big stone arch. It was built from the stone "tenelija" which came from the quarry in Mukoša, 5 km south of Mostar. It is 4,49 m wide, while the height from the summer water level is 21 m. The bridge was built of square stones connected with iron hooks and cast in lead. The well-known builders and masons from Dubrovnik and the surroundings of Popovo Polje built it. On the cornerstone on the left bank of the river, there is the following inscription in Arabic: KUDRET KEMERI – Strength of water.

The Old Bridge was built at the narrowest part of the Neretva canyon, and it thus completed the whole marvellous picture of this landscape making it one of the most

⇦ *Mostar, the centre of the old town with its "stone crescent" bridge, forts and towers* beautiful in the whole length of the Neretva, from its source to the Adriatic Sea. Every passer-by stops here to admire this masterpiece of Turkish Arab architecture. Mostar is known for its bridge all over Europe and the world. The central part of the old town, with its forts, towers and gates, developed around this magnificent monument producing an unique architectural whole.

The renewed Old Bridge was inaugurated on July 23, 2004. The World Bank and UNESCO were included in the renovation, while the constructor was the Turkish firm ER-BU.

**The Tower of Halebija or Ćelovina** – It is on the right bank of the Neretva next to the Old Bridge. There was a prison on the ground-floor from 1716, while the floors above served as guard-houses for the accommodation of the garrison.

**The Tower of Tara** – This is on the left side of the Old Bridge. It was built semi-circular in shape with its flat side turned towards the Bridge. The walls are more than three metres thick. Erected in 1676, it served as a store house for gun-powder and ammunition until Austro-Hungarian occupation in 1878.

**The Tower of Herceguša** – This is near the Tower of Tara. It was most probably built in the first half of the 15th century, while the first chain bridge still existed. Herceg Stjepan Vukčić-Kosača built it.

**The Asker Mosque** – This mosque was erected near the Old Bridge, next to the left bank of the Neretva between 1512 and 1520 by order of the sultan Jazuv Selim. The mosque has no minaret, a flat roof,

*Mostar, beauty of nature, plus the imagination of ancient builders*

and was mostly used as a place of worship ("mesdžid") for soldiers who guarded the Bridge.

**Kriva Ćuprija** – A hundred metres from the confluence of the Radobolja and the Neretva, there was a single-arched stone bridge under the name of Kriva Ćuprija which was destroyed in 1996 due to a very high water level together with a strong current. It was built by Ćejvan Kethoda before 1558.

**Hadži-Kurt's Mosque or Taba-čica Mosque** – This lies on the right side of the Neretva, a little more than 100 metres from the Old Bridge, not far from the Tower of Halebija. It was built before 1600 of cut stone and it was covered with stone tiles on the four-gabled roof. Its minaret, next to the right wall, is 20 meters high. A rivulet from the river Radobolja flows under the mosque and it joins the Neretva to the south of the Old Bridge. The mosque was mostly used by tanners ("tabaci") who were janissaries by origin.

**Ćejvan-Ćehaj's Mosque** – Of square shape it is next to the left bank of the Neretva, in the immediate vicinity of the Old Bridge, on the main road ("Velika Tepa"). It is thought to be one of the oldest buil-

*Kriva Ćuprija (Aslant Bridge), one of the oldest buildings of Oriental architecture from 1558*

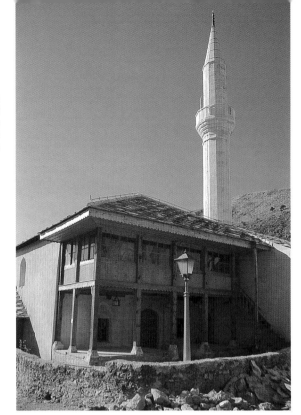

*Mostar, the mosque Tabačica, built around 1600 is covered by stone tiles*

*Mostar, Sahat-kula from 1636, the sound of its bells is unforgettable*

dings in Mostar from 1552/1553, confirmed by an inscription above the entrance gate. The minaret was added next to the left wall near the entrance.

**Sahat-kula** – Its square base measures 3,45 metres and it is 15 metres high. According to the letter of thanks of Ibrahim Šarić from 1636, it is evident that it existed even before. Evlija Ćelebija states that the bell sound from this mosque can be heard three hours walking distance away. The folk song says that Sahat-kula was built by Fatima-kaduna Šarić. The vizier of Herzegovina, Ali-pasha Rizvanbe-

*Mostar, the unique Koski Mehmed-pasha's mosque built in 1617 on a rocky bank of the Neretva*

govíć ordered the bell for this tower, 250 kg in weight, from the Zadar vice-Regent in 1838. The Austro-Hungarian authorities made use of it for war purposes. The tower was returned to its original function in 1981.

**Koski Mehmed-pasha's Mosque** – This is 150 metres to the north of the Old Bridge, on the bank of the Neretva between Mala Tepa and Kujunžiluk. It is of square shape (12,4 x 12,4 metres) and covered by a dome. Its minaret is only a few metres from the bank of the Neretva without any decoration below the gallery ("šerefa"). The Mosque was completed in 1618/1619, while the blessing of the ground ("uvakufljenje") was done seven years before. The fountain ("šedrvan") in front of the Mosque was set under six stone columns, connected with arches, and covered with stone tiles.

*Mostar, "šadrvan" in front of Koski Mehmed-pasha's mosque*

*The interior Koski Mehmed-Pasha's mosque*

*Mostar, the interior of Karadoz-bey's mosque*

**Karađoz-bey's Mosque** – This is the most important monumental work of Islamic sacred architecture in the 16th century in the whole territory of Herzegovina. There is a dome above the Mosque and its interior area is square (13,4 x 13,4 m). Its minaret is tall and harmonious, decorated with stalactites under the gallery. The Mosque was completed in 1557. During the Second World War it was severely damaged. It is the work of the Turkish architect Kodža Mimara Sinan, and probably the stone masters from Dubrovnik built it. The fountain is in the courtyard in front of the Mosque. From the courtyard, one can enter the building of the "medresa" which has a library.

**Nasuh-aga Vučjaković's Mosque** – In the main street on the left bank of the Neretva. It is also known under the name "The Mosque under the Lime-tree". It is domed and dates probably from 1564. The tablet built in above the entrance says it was erected in 1528/29. However, this date is suspect as the form of letters is not from that time.

**The Old Mosque** – The Old Mosque, next to the Old Bridge, has been preserved with all the ancillary buildings dating from the 15th to the 19th centuries. This urban group has all the characteristics of the Turkish age. Nearby, there is a series of small craft workshops and handicrafts shops ("čepenci" and "magaze"), as well as small restaurants offering traditional specialities. This part of the town is a favourite promenade for young people, artists and tourists,

*Mostar, "šadrvan" in the middle of the courtyard in front of Karađoz-bey's mosque*

because they can experience here the attractions of the Orient on a small scale.

*Mostar, Nasuh-aga Vučjaković's mosque or "The Mosque under the Lime-tree"*

*"Turbe" is a specially marked tomb of well-known personaliies dating from Turkish times ("Krehino turbe")*

**Tepa-pijaca** – The main Mostar market place has been called for centuries "Tepa" or "Small Tepa", and it is situated in the immediate vicinity of Kujundžiluk Street and the Old Bridge.

Here, you can also find various handicrafts by local craftsmen and food specialities (for example, cheese).

**Bišćević's House (Ćošak)** – One of the most significant and most beautiful houses from Turkish times. It is situated in Bišćević Street, on the very banks of the Neretva. It was built in the 18th century with a ground-floor and one floor above where there is a large room for conversation ("divan-han"). In the courtyard, there is a small building which served as a

*Mostar, Čardak-kula next to the Old Bridge, a precious building from Turkish times*

*Tepa, the main market of Mostar where one trades, talks and meets other people*

*Mostar, Nezir-aga's mosque*

kitchen. The interior is arranged in oriental style, and the floor is extended on poles. The facade is characteristic of Turkish architecture of that time. A small collection of household objects is arranged in the house.

**Kajtaz's House** – This house is in the street of the same name and it was most probably built at the end of the 16th or at the beginning of the 17th century. It belongs to town dwelling architecture and it is the most beautiful living complex with separate houses for men and women. High walls protect it from strong sunshine and from people on the outside looking in. Valuable carpets can be seen on the floors of large rooms, and numerous books in Arabic have been preserved.

**Ćorović's House** – The bir-

*Mostar, the Turkish House or Bišćevića-ćošak built in 1635*

*Mostar's Turkish House: a valuable example of Oriental dwelling architecture*

*Mostar, the shady courtyard of the Turkish House, an area for rest and talk*

*Mostar, Kajtaz's House from the 18th century fenced in by a high wall to protect its inhabitants from the curious gazes of the outside world*

*Mostar, Kajtaz's House, a valuable cluster of buildings from Turkish times*

*Mostar, Kajtaz's House; with items of everyday use*

*Mostar, Alajbegović's House built in 1876*

*Mostar, the new Orthodox church was a monumental edifice built in 1873 (destroyed in the war of 1992/1995)*

th-place of the writer Svetozar Ćorović. It was built in stone in the similar way that most Dalmatian houses were built at that time (1874). The writer Aleksa Šantić lived and worked in this house, and his room

*Mostar, a precious icon to Our Lady in the old Orthodox church*

with the library and his manuscripts can be seen.

**Muslibegović's House** – It was built in 1876 in what is now the street of Osman Đikić at Brankovac. This is probably the most recent house from Turkish times, and it consists of a ground-floor and a first floor, while the courtyard is surrounded with a high wall. A very nicely furnished "divanhana" is on the first floor.

**The Old Orthodox Church** – An even older church had been built at the place of the present Old Orthodox Church; this was destroyed in order to build this beautiful church in 1833. There is a very

valuable icon of Our Lady in the interior of the church, together with numerous icons of Russian, Venetian and local production from the 15th to the 19th centuries.

**The New Orthodox Church** – The building of this church in the immediate vicinity of the old one began in 1863 and it was completed in the autumn of 1873. Most of the money for its building was given by the Mostar Orthodox Christians, while Sultan Abdul-Aziz gave 10,000 groschens.

**The Catholic Church** – There was a Franciscan monastery at Zahum in Mostar in 1533, which was destroyed by the Turks at the

*Mostar, this big modern Catholic cathedral was built in 1980, not far from the Bishop's Residence*

end of the 16th century. From that year until 1847, Catholics did not have their own church in Mostar. They then built the church of Sts Peter and Paul. Mostar became the seat of the Catholic bishops in the middle of the 19th century.

The old diocese building was built at Vukodol surrounded by a high wall above which there is a stone tablet with an inscription showing the year of building, 1847. The bishops and the Franciscan school had their headquarters there. The first Bishop of Herzegovina, f. Rafo Barišić separated Herzegovina from Bosna Srebrena.

*Đuro Seder, The Last Supper (1,88 x 4,76 m), oil painting on canvas, 1989*

*Omer Mujadžić, Pietà, oil painting on canvas, 1980*

Due to f. Franjo Miličević a printing office began work in this building. The Catholic church was within
the old diocese complex until 1866
when a new Catholic church was
completed at Podhum, in what was
previously the garden of the Vizier
Ali-pasha Rizvanbegović of Herzegovina. In the interior of the church
there is a memorial bas-relief of
Bishop Paškal Buconjić, the work of
the sculptor Ivan Rendić. The Franciscan monastery and the provincial
residence were built next to the
church. A rich collection of archives
of the Herzegovina friars is in the
monastery, encompassing the period
from 1554 until the present day, and
consists of documents, reports, letters, etc. in various languages, from
Western to Oriental. There is a special collection of several hundred

Mostar, the Franciscan monastery, the manuscript of an Arab-Persian-Turkish dictionary from 1464

Oriental manuscripts, of which the oldest date from the 15th century.

The well-known monastery library houses almost 50,000 books with some very rare editions.

The Franciscan monastery holds also a big collection of paintings, ranging from the Italian masters of the 16th and 17th centuries to modern avant-garde artists.

The Franciscan church was completely destroyed in May 1992 dur-

Mostar, the Franciscan monastery, Our Lady and the Child, an unknown Baroque master (after Raphael's Madonna della Seggiola)

*Mostar, the Franciscan monastery, The Dream of St Joseph, an unknown 18th C Italian master*

ing the last war, together with part of the monastery, which is now completely restored while the renovation of the church is in progress. Enormous cultural treasure, archives, the library and collections of works of art were protected from devastation during the war.

**The Synagogue** – The believers in Judaism built a synagogue, which was destroyed and rebuilt, and which was donated to the Puppet Theatre by the Sephardis and Ashkenazis.

**The Jewish Cemetery** – There are three hundred graves at Zalik with sarcophagi of limestone and the Hebrew star and letters. A small monument fenced in by steel bars holds the body of the beautiful girl Simha who died from tuberculosis when she was twenty years old. Some of the tombstones are written in German. Tourists from all over

*Mostar, the Franciscan monastery, Vlaho Bukovac: A Woman of Dubrovnik*

the world visit this cemetery and some of them place a small stone on Simha's tomb; this is a thousand year old custom.

**Old families of Mostar** – F. Pavo Dragičević supplied the scientist Vladimir Ćorović with the data of the old families of Mostar. The old registry of deaths from 1832 to 1848 says: "Of all these mentioned, only Vujica and Bojčić are old families of Mostar, and all others are immigrants."

The following old Catholic families are mentioned there: Šoići (1717), Karapandžići or Pandže (1723), Zelenika (1742); and in the first half of the 19th century: Barišić, Horeč, Mitrović, Soptić, Arapović, Doko, Čule, Vujica, Dugandžić, Šarić, Bakula, etc.

Many of the Muslim families from Mostar had Turkish names although they did not speak Turkish:

*Mostar, Bishop's Residence built in 1906*

Džudže, Kajtazi, Ćumurije, Temimi, Ćevre, Kolukčije, Taslamani, Ćišić, etc.

The Orthodox families were: Šotrići, Pamučine, Jovan Zec, Risto Bjelobrk, Škiljevići, Milakovići, Putice, Pejdići, Đurići, Kablari.

**The Cathedral** – The cathedral was built at Balinovac in 1980 beside the new building of the Diocese built in 1906. The interior of the cathedral is embellished with a stained-glass window by Ivo Dulčić and a mosaic by Zdenko Grgić. The ca-

*Mostar, Rondo, a round square, the most beautiful square of the new Mostar*

thedral and its stained-glass windows were destroyed in the war of 1992/1995. Renovation is in progress.

**Hamam (Turkish baths)** – It is covered with 6 domes and an extended ceiling built of stone; situated in the vicinity of the Old Bridge it was most probably built in the second part of the 16th century.

Šejh Jujino Turbe (a domed burial site) – It stands on 6 stone columns joined with arches and covered with a dome. Turbe was built in 1831.

**The Military cemetery,** from 1879, is near the Buna-Blagaj crossroads. All soldiers killed in the vicinity of Mostar and who had lived under the Austro-Hungarian Monarchy were buried there. There is a

*Mostar, Šejh Jujino Turbe, built in 1831, the tomb of Mustafa Ejubović, a well-known Mostar writer*

*The Military Cemetery from 1879 in Mostar*

chapel next to the south wall, while an Italian one is next to the northern wall, and was erected in 1942/43, with a large cross.

The military cemetery is under the protection of the Hague convention as an international military cemetery where soldiers taking part in fighting in this area during the Second World War were buried.

**The Monument to Osman Đikić** – This was erected next to the entrance to Karadozbeg's Mosque. It is domed and it was made by the architect Aleksandar Derok.

**The Memorial Museum "Džemal Bijedić"** – The birth-place of the previous President of the Yugoslav government, Džemal Bijedić, has been arranged as a memorial museum remembering the life of

*Mostar, monument to the writer Osman Đikić*

*Mostar, the old Grammar School (1898), with numerous Moorish elements on its facade*

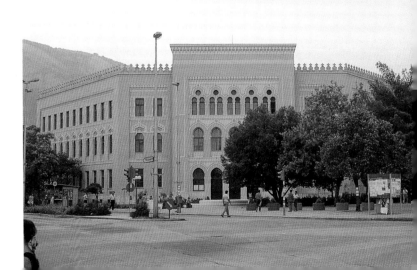

*The Music Centre, donated to Mostar by a group of famous musicians led by the renowned tenor Luciano Pavarotti*

that great statesman.

Rondo – This round square was built during the Austro-Hungarian administration which lasted from 1878 to 1918. Six avenues planted with plane-trees and lime-trees extend from it. Their shade attracts numerous visitors and also the people of Mostar during the hot summer days.

**Gojko Vuković's House** – It was opened in 1984, and depicts the life and work of this outstanding leader of the workers' movement in Mostar and Herzegovina.

**The Grammar School, the "Neretva" hotel and Public Baths** were built during the Austro-Hungarian administration. These buildings are built in pseudo-Moorish style with some elements of Oriental architecture.

*Mostar, the Town Baths ("Banja") built in 1912*

*Mostar, the "Bristol" hotel*

*Mostar, the "Ero" hotel*

*Mostar, the "Bevanda" hotel*

*Mostar, the "Mostar" hotel*

*Mostar, the Town Hall*

**The monument to Aleksa Šantić** – Not far from Ćorović's house in the park, there is the monument to the poet Aleksa Šantić in front of the former "magaza" – the shop of his father Risto. The memorial is the work of the academician painter Nikola Janković.

**The Partisans' Memorial Cemetery** is the work of the famous architect Bogdan Bogdanović, built in 1965. The people of Mostar thus paid tribute to their sons and daughters killed in the People's Liberation Antifascist War. The monument is set on a terrace-like terrain and is covered with grass and floral areas.

ILIĆI – Formerly it was a village, now it is the western suburb of Mostar, well known for its cherries which ripen at the end of April.

*The People's Theatre in Mostar*

*Mostar, the Medresa, connecting the spirit of time with the spirit of man*

CIM – The remains of a late Hellenic bishop's basilica from the 5/6$^{th}$ centuries were found in Cim in the location of Crkvina.

POTOCI – The remains of a Roman settlement with a late Hellenic basilica have been preserved in Potoci near Mostar. Two sarcophagi contain female jewellery from East Goths in the 6$^{th}$ century.

*Croatian home of Herceg Stjepan Kosača*

# THE NERETVA CANYON

*The canyon of the clear blue-green and Neretva*

A magnificent and deep canyon is cut deep down to the Neretva river bed between Jablanica and Mostar, some ten kilometres between the massifs of the Čvrsnica and Prenj mountains. The massifs consist of steeply inclined layers of rock thrown up by geological formations. The canyon is full of brooks and water sources which rush towards the waters of the Neretva making attractive cascades on their way. Several belvederes have been arranged along the communications road.

## SHOOTING AND FISHING

### SHOOTING

Shooting various bigger and smaller game is well developed in the near and farther surroundings of Mostar, in upland woods, lowland pastures and bare Karst. Shooting

*Cattle breeding – an important branch of economy*

mostly the larger game, is especially popular in the areas of the Crna Gora, Čabulja, Prenj, Čvrsnica, and Velež mountains. The shooting season lasts from June to December. Huts and lodges for rest and shelter have been built in various shooting areas. Sportsmen go from Mostar and Nevesinje to the mountains of Velež and Crna Gora to shoot bear, deer and chamois, and from Mostar, Jablanica, and Konjic to the areas of Prenj and Čvrsnica to shoot mouflon, chamois, bear, deer and grouse.

Partridge and hare are mostly shot in the areas of Dubrava, Podveležje, and Žegulja. Accommodation for gun sportsmen is available in Mostar, Stolac and other towns in Herzegovina.

The shooting area of Hutovo Blato abounds in water fowl. Accommodation is available in the hotels in Karaotok and Čapljina, which are connected with game areas by easily accessible roads.

The association of gun sportsmen issues the permits.

The "Prenj" shooting area – This area for large game comprises 55,000 hectares of the Prenj mountain. It is half an hour's drive away from Mostar. There is organised shooting of roe-deer, chamois, bear, mouflon, and wild boar, also Greek partridge and grouse. The mountain air is beneficial for the human organism due to the sudden change of the air's density.

Diva Grabovica – One of the most beautiful mountain areas and canyons in this part of Europe.

The "Busak" shooting reserve comprises 11,000 hectares and is situated in the mountainous area of Velež. It is the best known shooting area for Greek partridge.

*Enjoying angling in the Neretva or in some of the lakes, streams or smaller rivers*

## FISHING

Fishing for anglers is organised in the area of Mostar and its surroundings on the river Neretva, lakes and water accumulations, the tributaries of the Neretva and various streams.

The following artificial lakes are very popular for fishing: Jablaničko, Ramsko, Grabovica, Salakovac and Vrapčić, and also the natural Boračko Lake. The rivers Ljuta, Rakitnica, Rama, Doljanka, Drežanjak, Grabovka, Radobolja, Jasenica, and Trebižat flow into the Neretva from the right-hand side, while the Bijela, Buna with Bunica and Bregava flow into it from the other side. All these artificial and natural lakes as well as rivers with their numerous streams are rich in various fish, especially in trout.

Fishing associations issue fishing permits (both daily and annual) in every town.

Fishing is permitted from April 1 to October 30.

# THE SURROUNDINGS OF MOSTAR

The surroundings of Mostar abound in archaeological finds of human habitations: Badanj in the canyon of the Bregava (from the Palaeolithic); The Green Cave above the spring of the Buna; Peć-Mlini near Grude from the Neolithic; the Varvara habitation near Prozor (from the Stone Age), then Blagaj, Hodbina, Gornji Polog and others which were inhabited even in Roman times until the 4th century. There are interesting burial grounds with decorated upstanding tomb-stones ("stećci"). Among the bigger necropolises are Bučići (165 tombs), Rančići (100), Padežina in two locations with more than 80 tombs, while 52 are at Kruševo near Mostar, of which 19 are decorated.

## BLAGAJ

Medieval Stjepan-grad lies twelve kilometres south of Mostar. It is raised on a crag of the mount Hum,

after which the whole of Herzegovina was called Hum or Zahumlje before the arrival of the Turks. The hill-fort of the Illyrian tribe of the Daorsi is supposed to have been here until the 2nd century, and after that a Roman fortification. There was probably a church in the old part of the town, in the courtyard to the left of the entrance. A new fortification was built in the 6th century on the ruins of the Roman one. It was mentioned under the name of Bona in the 10th century by the Byzantine Emperor and chronicler Constantin Porphyrogenitus. The Bosnian feudal family Kosača renovated the town in the 15th century, building four well-fortified towers and numerous embrasures. The last local master of Hum, Herceg Stjepan Vukčić Kosača resided there. The Turks occupied the town in 1466.

The source of the river Buna, one of the fastest flowing in Europe, is in Blagaj below Stjepan-grad. Water

*The remains of medieval Stjepan-grad*

*Blagaj, a detail of the dervish's Moslem house ("tekija") at the source of the Buna river*

gushes down from a huge cave in the sheer rock, above which many birds build their nests at a height of 25 metres. The species are various, from golden eagle to rock pigeons. An old Muslim monastery ("Derviška Tekija") was built at the base of the rock. This attractive religious and cultural building was built at the end of the 15th or the beginning of the 16th centuries. The building houses a mill, built in the style of Turkish Baroque, a Turkish bath and installed heating appliances under the floor. "Tekija" is open to visitors as a museum demonstrating an older way of life.

Several well-preserved flour mills exist next this complex, together with a fish-farm. The Green Cave above the Buna spring is an archaeological location belonging to the Western Mediterranean Neo-lithic era (3,000 – 2,800 BC).

The Emperor's Mosque dates from the middle of the 16th century. Kolaković's House is especially interesting due to its large room on the first floor, decorated with wood carvings. The complex of Velagić's buildings from the 18th century is also very interesting.

## BUNA

The vizier of Herzegovina Ali-pasha Rizvanbegović ordered a mosque to be built at Buna. A tread-mill ("dolap") and several old water mills have been preserved.

Buna is a well-known excursion point for the men and women of Mostar attracting them with its natural beauties, abundance of water, fishing possibilities, shaded paths and other pleasant areas.

*Međugorje, the parish church of St Jacob, a place for gathering and praying for many pilgrims*

## MEĐUGORJE

The name Međugorje is of Slavonic origin after the location of this town between steep hills. The area of Međugorje, and the broader area of Brotanj, belonged to the district ("ager") of Narona. Examples of Greek coins have been preserved; they probably came here through merchandise. A Roman settlement, with an early basilica, has been discovered in the location of Srebrenica. Several smaller archaeological finds belong to this period, as well as many examples of Roman coins.

Međugorje was mentioned at the sharia court in Mostar in 1633/34 during several court cases in which the people of Međugorje were involved. The remains of several towers from Turkish times have been preserved: Hrnjić's tower (today in

*Peace and quiet at Podbrdo, where the apparition of Our Lady first took place*

*Pilgrims at Križevac*

the possession of the Sivrić family), the towers of Hadžići, Topalovići, Voljevica, and others.

The warm Mediterranean climate penetrates along the Neretva river to this region, so that Mediterranean crops are cultivated here. The red earth (*terra rossa*) from Međugorje and Brotanj benefits the cultivation of excellent Herzegovina tobacco and grapes.

The first elementary school was opened in 1903/1904.

Međugorje is well connected with its near and distant surroundings.

After 1981, Međugorje became the best known and most visited place of pilgrimage in this part of Europe.

Our Lady appeared to a group of boys and girls from Međugorje on June 24, 1981. Since then, She has appeared every day, and Međugorje has become an unique phenomenon attracting thousands of pilgrims from all over the world.

The parish church of St James is the central point of worship for pilgrims to Međugorje who listen to Our Lady's messages.

Mount Križevac rises one kilometre away from the church in Međugorje. A reinforced concrete cross was built there in 1934 to the "memory of 1900 years of Christ's Passion". It is 8,56 m high.

Međugorje is 29 km away from Mostar.

*Žitomislić, the 17th century Royal Doors in the church of the Annunciation*

## ŽITOMISLIĆ

The ruins of a complex with a double church and a protected courtyard from the 5th or 6th centuries can be found in the village of Žitomislić, at Crkvina, in the valley along the left bank of the Neretva.

An Orthodox monastery and church from the 16th century are on the left bank of the Neretva 17 km to the south of Mostar. A valuable iconostasis, old icons and valuable manuscripts have been preserved in them. The monastery was destroyed in the last war (1992 – 1995).

*Široki Brijeg, the impressive church of the Assumption of the Blessed Virgin Mary which holds valuable art treasures*

## ŠIROKI BRIJEG

This picturesque small town is 21 km from Mostar. The small river Lištica flows through it and has its source under the limestone rocks at the foot of the Čabulja mountain. At this spring, there are several mills for rolling linen as water temperature never varies. The river is rich in trout, and the whole area abounds in small game and birds. On the hill above the small town, there is a Franciscan monastery built in 1846. A magnificent church to Our Lady is next to the monastery. A pastoral centre, a rich art gallery, a Grammar School, and the Academy of arts are among the more important institutions in Široki Brijeg.

## POČITELJ

The remains of a medieval town can be found on a steep limestone hill, next to the left bank of the Neretva, some thirty kilometres to the south of Mostar.

The Croatian-Hungarian King Matija Korvin suggested that Herceg Stjepan Kosača fortify the town before the arrival of Turkish danger, so the fortification began in 1465. However, the Turks occupied this important strategic point on the Neretva in 1471. They also gave it its present appearance during the 17th and 18th centuries. Among valuable buildings of Oriental architecture there are: Dadži-Alija's Mosque, Gavran-Kapetanović's House, Šišman-Ibrahim-pasha's Medresa, Sahat-kula, Han, and Haman; they were all severely damaged during the last war (1992 –1995).

*Počitelj, an unique 'museum-town'*

## HUTOVO BLATO

This is situated to the south-east of Čapljina, at 1-4 metres above sea level and consists of Svitavsko and Deransko Blato divided by the limestone massif of Ostrvo (123-312 metres above sea level). The river Krupa flows from Deransko Lake, and receives from Svitavsko Blato its tributary Matica, below the village of Drečevo, it then flows into the river Neretva. In 1979, the reversible hydro-electric plant Čapljina was built, and an artificial lake had to be created for this purpose from Svitava to Sjekos, about 10 km long and plenty of water all the year. Flocks of wild duck, geese, coots and other birds stay permanently in the area of Blato due to the mild Mediterranean climate penetrating along the Neretva from the Adriatic Sea. More than 250 species of wading birds spend the winter here. There are also various fish, particularly eel and carp.

Hutovo Blato is a well-known nature reserve of migratory birds. It is registered as a natural rarity and protected by law.

*Hutovo blato, nature reserve for birds and various fish*

## KARAOTOK

This lies on a hill, to the left of the asphalted road Čapljina-Metković, near the village of Klepci, in dense coniferous woods. This is the starting-off point for game sportsmen and anglers to go to Svitava and Deransko Blato. Tourists can visit the reserve Hutovo Blato in small boats. Travel agencies from Dubrovnik and other coastal towns bring them by coach to enjoy the beauty of an untouched, wild and attractive landscape.

## MOGORJELO

Mogorjelo is known for its late classical culture. It got its name from the Christian martyr Heramog – Mogor to whom a church was consecrated, built on the remains of a Roman *villa rustica*. It lies on the right

*Sightseeing in the picturesque landscape of the Hutovo blato reserve*

bank of the Neretva, one kilometre to the south of Čapljina, surrounded by cypress trees which give it a special charm. An archaeological site was discovered there and excavations were carried out from 1899 to 1903. There was a country estate here in and 1st and 2nd centuries which was probably burned down in the 3rd century. A bigger agricultural estate was formed later, at the end of the 3rd or the beginning of the 4th century, with a two storey building and agricultural plant (a refinery, a bakery, a wine cellar, stores, etc). This *villa rustica* was probably destroyed between 401 and 403, when the West Goths passed through this region from Greece to Italy.

Mogorjelo was most probably abandoned in the first half of the 5th century. However at the end of the fifth century, two early Christian basilicas were built here, which were destroyed during the great migrations of the people.

## THE KRAVICA CASCADES

They are on the river Trebižat, seven kilometres to the south-east of Ljubuški. This is a magnificent natural phenomenon which attracts many visitors, and the cascades are thought to be the most beautiful in Herzegovina. They are 26 metres high and about 120 metres wide, in a semi-circular shape built of travertine. Many people come to swim under them in summer time. Several water mills for grinding wheat, and mills for rolling linen have been preserved nearby.

⇨ *Badanj, the proof of Palaeolithic man's artistic creativity*

*The magnificent strength and beauty of the Kravica cascades*

*Radimlja, an unique medieval graveyard of upright tombstones ("stećci")*

## BADANJ

Badanj is the only fortified habitation of Palaeolithic man in the canyon of the river Bregava. This find in a semi-cave is from 12,000 to 16,000 years old, and examples of stone tools and the remains of animal's bones were found here. The first proof regarding the art of the Palaeolithic man was also found in this semi-cave: a damaged engraving on an oblique flat stone depicting a horse attacked with arrows.

## RADIMLJA

Radimlja lies three kilometres to the west of Stolac, in the Vidovo Field, near the communications road Mostar-Stolac-Trebinje. This is the most significant and the most beautiful cemetery of medieval upright tomb-stones. It has 133 tomb-stones, of which three crosses, 37 tablets, 33 gable-tombs and 60 coffins remain. 63 tombs are decorated with various motifs in bas-re-

lief, with fine chiselling. The most numerous motifs are those of curling trefoil, ribbons, shields with swords, bows and arrows, lances, maces, crosses, and human and animal figures. The inscriptions on these huge tombstones are written in Bosnian cyrillc script ("bosančica").

## OŠANIĆI

The remains of a town settlement of the Illyrian tribe of Daorsi are above the river Radimlja to the north-west of Stolac. Huge dry-stone walls of enormous stone blocks, several metres long, coins with the inscription "Daorson", fragments of ceramics and the remains of ash point to the Greek influence and a rich life in this ancient town, and also that it was interrupted by force.

## NEUM

Neum, a well developed tourist resort, lies to the south-east of the mouth of the Neretva, in a deep protected bay, to the south of the small town of Klek on the Adriatic Highway.

The Turks as the then rulers of Bosnia obtained through the Treaty of Požarevac of 1718 an exit to the sea at the frontier between Venetian Dalmatia to the north and the Republic of Dubrovnik to the south.

Neum is today an attractive tourist destination, with modern hotels "Neum", "Sunce", "Zenit", "Tat", and "Stela", and beautifully arranged beaches. The folklore ensemble under the name of "Linđo", with its rich programme of songs and dances entertain guests during the tourist season. Several Turkish guns, which were set in the nearby fortifications, are exhibited on a beach in Neum.

Hutovo lies not far from Neum. An important fortification was erected on the pass between Popovo and Žaba in ancient times and was used until recently. It protected the only route from the sea to the interior of Herzegovina. The majority of these fortified buildings were built by the Venetians during their war against the Turks, in which the Turks later put their own garrison. Hustovski Town was further enlarged at the time of Hadžibeg Rizvanbegović and it became then the headquarters of the military district.

A lapidary of archaeological remains has been arranged in the courtyard of the parish church, and the County Offices were built.

In Hrasno, in the hinterland of Neum, there is the Shrine of the Queen of Peace with valuable religious artefacts, and also a County Museum and a Gallery with sacred, historical and general exhibits.

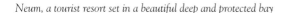

*Neum, a tourist resort set in a beautiful deep and protected bay*

# TOURIST INFORMATION

**TOURIST BOARD HNK-HNŽ (Croatian-Neretva County – Croatian-Neretva Canton)**, Mostar, Dr. A. Starčevića b.b., tel. 397-350, fax: 397-351
**MOSTAR**: Area code: 036; Area code for the Federation od BiH 00387
**HOTELS**: Bevanda★★★★, Stara Ilička b.b., tel. 332-332, fax. 315-693; Ero★★★, Dr. Ante Starčevića b.b., 386-777, fax. 386-700; Bristol★★★, M. Bataljona b.b. 500-100, fax. 500-502; Mostar★★★, Kneza Domagoja b.b. 322-679, fax. 315-693
Private accommodation: **TOURIST INFORMATION CENTRE** tel. 580-833
**TOURIST INFORMATION**: Fortuna Trade Tours Mosta – branch office 1 (The main railway station) and Private Accommodation, tel: 036/552-197, tel./fax: 036/551-888, tel/fax: 036/551-887, 386-710; www.fortuna.ba
e-mail: fortuna@cob.net.ba
**RENT A CAR**: LV – Long Visus, K.M.V. Humskog 57/Rondo, 88 000 Mostar tel: 036/323-700
**IMPORTANT TELEPHONE NUMBERS**: Road Service: 1282; Police. 122; Firemen: 123; Emergency Service: 124; Railway Station/Information: 551-956; Bus Information: 036/552-025
**HOSPITALS**: Klinička bolnica Mostar, Ulica kardinala Stepinca bb, tel: 036/313-238; RMC "Dr. Safet Mujić", Južni logor bb, tel: 036/576-910/576-911
**AIRPORT**: Ortiješ bb, tel: 036/350-212

# CONTENTS

**MOSTAR – AN AREA RICH IN CULTURE AND CONTACTS OF CIVILISATION, 5**
**CLIMATE AND GEOGRAPHY, 14**
**OLD SETTLEMENTS, 16**
**TRADE AND HANDICRAFTS IN TURKISH TIMES, 20**
**THE HISTORY OF MOSTAR, 22**
Turkish Rule and its Decline, 27
**CULTURAL AND HISTORICAL HERITAGE, 32**
**THE NERETVA CANYON, 60**
**SHOOTING AND FISHING, 60**
Shooting, 60 / Fishing, 61
**THE SURROUNDINGS OF MOSTAR, 62**
Blagaj, 62 / Buna, 63 / Međugorje, 64 / Žitomislić, 66 / Široki Brijeg, 66 / Počitelj, 67 / Hutovo Blato, 67 / Karaotok, 68 / Mogorjelo, 68 / The Kravica Cascades, 69 / Badanj, 70 / Radimlja, 70 / Ošanići, 70 / Neum, 70
**TOURIST INFORMATION, 72**

*The Partisans' Memorial Cemetery*